**Illustrator:**
Kathy Bruce

**Editor:**
Evan D. Forbes, M.S. Ed.

**Editor-in-Chief:**
Sharon Coan, M.S. Ed.

**Art Director:**
Elayne Roberts

**Cover Artist:**
Keith Vasconcelles

**Imaging:**
David Bennett

**Product Manager:**
Phil Garcia

# WORLD GEOGRAPHY SERIES
# NORTH AMERICA

### BASED ON NEW NATIONAL GEOGRAPHY STANDARDS

*(This series can be purchased as a complete volume
or as seven separate continent books.)*

**Publishers:**
Rachelle Cracchiolo, M.S. Ed.
Mary Dupuy Smith, M.S. Ed.

**Author:**

*Julia Jasmine, M.A.*

***Teacher Created Materials, Inc.***
P.O. Box 1040
Huntington Beach, CA 92647
**ISBN-1-55734-693-3**

*©1995 Teacher Created Materials, Inc.*        Made in U.S.A.

# Table of Contents

# Introduction

## What Has Happened to Geography?

Studies made during the last couple of decades show geography as a neglected science, even physical geography, its most traditional form. One of the suspected causes has been the higher priority of teaching subjects like math and science in the classroom. There have been many well-publicized surveys showing that people in the United States are not very well informed about the Earth they live on. Large numbers of people—including students on campuses of important universities where some of the best-publicized surveys have been conducted—were unable to identify the three largest countries on the North American continent, find Florida on a United States map, or name the oceans that border the United States on a world map. (Elementary school students love to hear about these surveys because if they are studying geography, they will be able to answer all of the questions that these college students cannot.)

During the years that the study of geography was being set aside in many of our schools in favor of other priorities, the whole focus of geography changed. Geography was once divided into two major categories: physical geography and human geography. Physical geography is concerned with the natural features of the earth (land, water, and climate), how they relate to each other, and the living organisms, including people, on the Earth. Physical geography has been divided into several categories: biogeography, climatology, geomorphology, oceanography, and soil geography. Human geography studies the patterns of human activity and how it relates to the environment around them. Human geography has been divided into several categories: cultural, economic, historical, political, population, social, and urban.

It was easy to compare and contrast geography with other sciences such as astronomy, which describes the Earth in relation to its position in space, and geology, which studies the Earth's structure and composition.

Today, however, geography is crossing into other sciences, as well. We are seeing it in cultural anthropology, demographics, ecology, economics, meteorology, sociology, and zoology. Although these remain separate sciences, the lines separating them are more blurry than ever before, and many new approaches to the study of geography are being advocated.

## GENIP—A National Project

In 1984, the Association of American Geographers (AAG) together with the National Council for Geographic Education (NCGE) published *Guidelines for Geographic Education: Elementary and Secondary Schools* in which they identified five fundamental themes of geography. These five themes were specifically designed and written to be used by teachers. (Crossland, 1994) In 1987, these two groups were joined by the American Geographical Society (AGS) and the National Geographic Society (NGS) to form the Geographic Education National Implementation Project (GENIP) for the purpose of implementing the aforementioned guidelines and improving the status and quality of geographic education in the United States.

# Introduction (cont.)

## What Has Happened to Geography? (cont.)

### The Five Themes

The first theme is called *Location: Position on the Earth's Surface.* There are two kinds of locations: absolute and relative. The absolute, or exact, location of any place on Earth can be specified by giving its latitude and longitude. The relative location of a place is given by describing its relationship to other places. Absolute location is like a street address. ("I live at 2100 Oak Lane, Smalltown, CA 98765.") Relative location is a more qualitative set of directions. ("I live in the white two-story house on the corner across from the tennis courts in the park.")

The second theme is *Place: Physical and Human Characteristics.* These are the characteristics that differentiate one place from another. They include physical characteristics like landforms, bodies of water, climate, and plant and animal life, as well as land use, architecture, language, religion, type of government, and even communication and transportation if they are unique.

The third theme is *Relationships Within Places: Humans and Their Environment.* Here we ask students to take a look at the ways in which people react with their environments. This is important in this age of ecological awareness when we are trying to make good choices about the Earth.

The fourth theme is *Movement: Humans Interacting on the Earth.* This theme focuses on human interdependence. This is where a more general and comprehensive look is taken at transportation and communication.

The fifth and last theme is entitled *Regions: How They Form and Change.* GENIP defines a region as an area with one or more common characteristics or features which give it a measure of unity and make it different from the surrounding areas. The geography of the United States is often divided into a consideration of its regions—Northeast, Southeast, Midwest, Southwest, Rocky Mountain, and Pacific.

### A New Mix

These themes are really a new mix of the old physical/human divisions. The first and fifth themes are more "physical" and the second and fourth more "human," while the third theme contains much of the material connected with our concern for the safety of the environment. The chief benefit of this approach may be the freshness it brings to one of the oldest of the academic disciplines. The themes themselves can be taught and discussed in any order or combination.

# Introduction *(cont.)*

## North America

This book was designed to present an overview of the geography of the continent of North America. It is divided into five sections to match the themes of the Geographic Education National Implementation Project (GENIP), an educational project backed by some of the nation's most prestigious geographers.

Each section contains a selection of teaching pages, maps, activities, interesting facts, review questions, and puzzles or games. A plan for using the material to construct a geography center is also included, as well as ideas for putting together a book as a culminating activity.

You will also find a glossary of specialized vocabulary used by geographers. This will make it easier for your students to talk about the world in which they live.

# A Word or Two About Maps

## Projections

The landforms shown on maps and globes do not look exactly alike. This is because it is just as hard to "peel" a globe and flatten the Earth's "skin" out into a map as it is to peel an orange and flatten out its skin to make a smooth, even surface. Even if you can get the skin off the orange in one piece, the top and bottom edges must be broken and spread out.

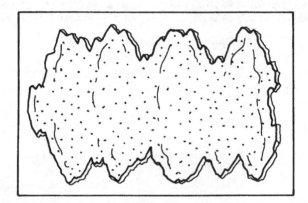

Different map makers (cartographers) have had different ideas about how to do this and have made different "projections." A projection is the way in which the map maker has chosen to flatten out the Earth's surface to make a flat map. Sometimes the map maker allows the breaks in Earth's surface to show.

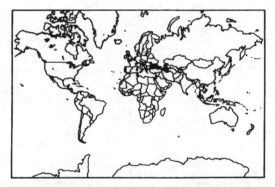

Sometimes the map maker stretches the Earth's "skin." This makes the countries near the poles look much bigger than they really are.

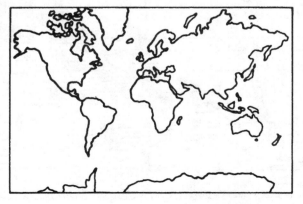

# A Word or Two About Maps (cont.)

## Projections (cont.)

Use your reference materials to find out the names of other common map projections and list them below. Research the advantages and disadvantages of each map projection you list and write them down below.

| Map Projection | Advantages | Disadvantages |
|---|---|---|
|  |  |  |
|  |  |  |
|  |  |  |
|  |  |  |
|  |  |  |
|  |  |  |
|  |  |  |
|  |  |  |
|  |  |  |
|  |  |  |
|  |  |  |
|  |  |  |
|  |  |  |
|  |  |  |
|  |  |  |
|  |  |  |
|  |  |  |
|  |  |  |
|  |  |  |

# A Word or Two About Maps *(cont.)*

## The Compass Rose

The compass rose is a small drawing that shows direction on a map. Most maps show north at the top and south at the bottom, west on the left and east on the right.

Look at maps to find some different styles of compass roses and then design your own. You can shrink your drawing and make multiple copies to use on the maps you make, color, or label.

# Where on Earth Is North America?

- North America extends from the cold Arctic Ocean to the warm Caribbean Sea.

- North America stretches from the Atlantic to the Pacific Oceans.

- North America is the third largest of the seven continents.

- North America contains the world's largest island.

Use these clues to find North America on this map. Color it blue.

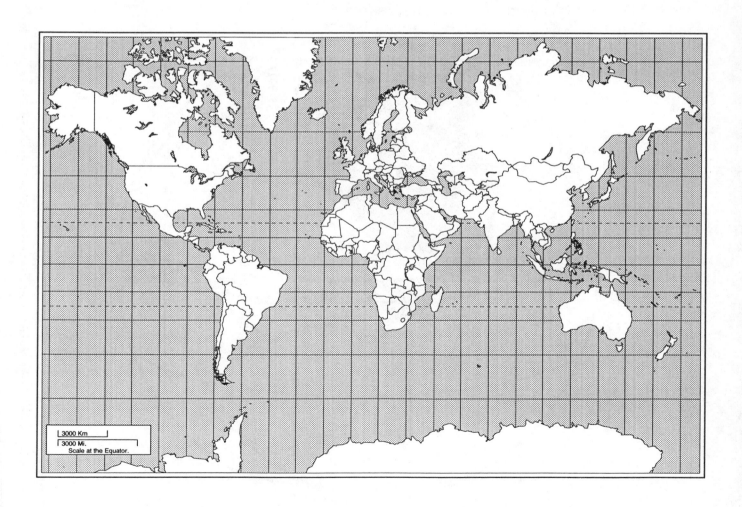

3000 Km
3000 Mi.
Scale at the Equator.

# Where on Earth Is North America? *(cont.)*

If you think of the Earth as a ball (a sphere or globe), you can draw a line around the middle (the equator) and separate the two halves into the top half (Northern Hemisphere) and the bottom half (Southern Hemisphere). Now you can talk about something as being in the Northern or Southern Hemisphere.

More lines are drawn around the Earth parallel to the equator and evenly spaced from the equator to the North and South Poles. They are called parallels or lines of latitude. They are numbered in degrees, starting with 0° at the equator and usually spaced at 15° intervals, ending with 90 ° N at the North Pole and 90° S at the South Pole.

(Geographers further divide their degrees into minutes and seconds so they can be very precise in locating the position of anything on the Earth's surface.)

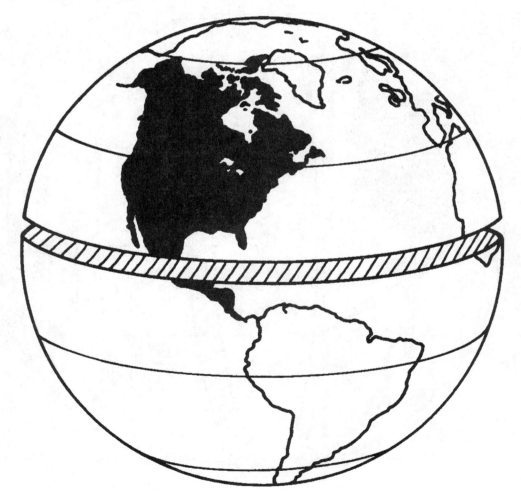

If you divide the Earth into its Northern and Southern Hemispheres, North America lies almost entirely in the_____Hemisphere.

# Where on Earth Is North America? *(cont.)*

You can also draw lines north and south around the Earth. These lines are called meridians or lines of longitude. They are usually shown 15° apart at the equator, but they all come together at the North and South Poles. (They also can be further divided into minutes and seconds just like the parallels.)

The line that runs through Greenwich, England, is called the prime meridian (0° ). Longitude is the distance east or west of the prime meridian. The line directly opposite the prime meridian is at 180° and is called the date line. If you are still thinking of the Earth as a ball (a sphere or globe), you can separate the two halves into the Western Hemisphere and the Eastern Hemisphere. (This is usually done along the meridians of 20° W and 160° E so all of Africa is in one hemisphere.)

If you divide the Earth into its Western and Eastern Hemispheres, North America is in the_____Hemisphere.

# Where on Earth Is North America? *(cont.)*

You can tell where things on the Earth are in two ways:

- You can give their exact or absolute location using latitude and longitude expressed in degrees (minutes and seconds).

- You can tell where they are in relation to other things.

Fill out the missing information to give the exact location of where you live:

| house number | street name | apartment number |
|---|---|---|
| city | state/country | zip code |

Now, use information from a map or globe to complete this description of the exact location of North America.

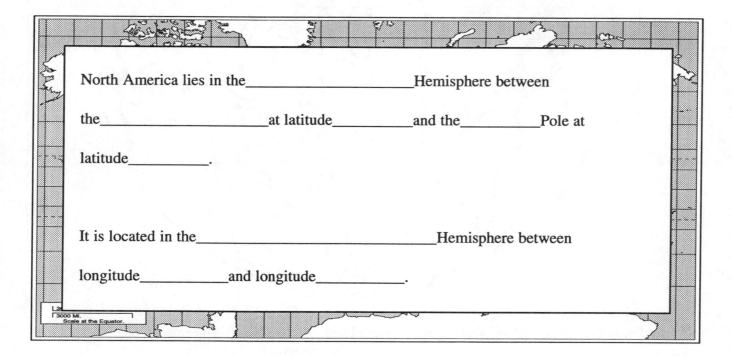

North America lies in the_____Hemisphere between

the_____at latitude_____and the_____Pole at

latitude_____.

It is located in the_____Hemisphere between

longitude_____and longitude_____.

# Where on Earth Is North America? *(cont.)*

You can tell where things on the Earth are in two ways:

- You can give their exact or absolute location using latitude and longitude expressed in degrees (minutes and seconds).

- You can tell where they are in relation to other things.

Fill out the missing information to give the location of where you live in relation to other things:

I live
between_____ and_____

near_____

and across
from_____ .

Now, use the information from a map or globe to complete this description of the relative location of North America.

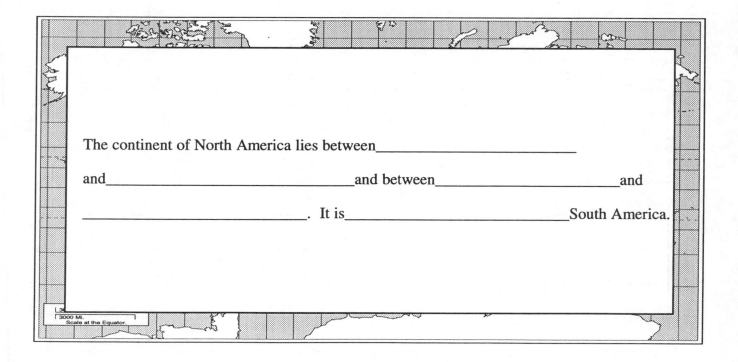

The continent of North America lies between_____

and_____ and between_____ and

_____ . It is_____ South America.

# Where in North America Is_____?

Use information from a globe or map, an atlas, an encyclopedia, and your geography book to write both the exact and relative locations of five of the countries on the North American continent. See the next page for the names of countries to choose from.

1. _____

   _____

   _____

   _____

   _____

2. _____

   _____

   _____

   _____

3. _____

   _____

   _____

   _____

4. _____

   _____

   _____

   _____

5. _____

   _____

   _____

   _____

# Countries, Departments, Dependencies, and Territories of North America

There are 36 countries, departments, dependencies, and territories of North America listed below. Find them forwards, backwards, and diagonally in the word search below.

```
G Q W F R E N C H O V E R S E A S D E P A R T M E N T S
R R E R T Y U A C O S T A R I C A I O P A S D F G H T T
E Z E X C V B N N M N Q T W E R T Y U I O P L K J P O V
N Z X E C V C A B N M D M R L K J H G F D S G A I A B I
A B P O N U U D T R E W U Q I Q A S D B F R G E H N A N
D A Z X C L B A A S Q W E R R N T Y A A E S R M D A G C
I R M N G U A T E M A L A V A C I H X N Z R A I S M O E
N B N Z X C V N B N M P O I U S A D A R E W M Q Q A A N
E A S E A S D F D G H S F D S M A D A W E R T U Y U J T
S D T P V O I U Y T E R E W A Q A A Z D X C V E D R T Y
N O K Q W I E R T T R E W S Q D O M I N I C A L A A S E
I S I Z X C S J A M A I C A C V B N M K J H G O W E R L
C W T E R N E T H E R L A N D S D E P E N D E N C I E S
A S T D F G S R B R I T I S H D E P E N D E N C I E S A
R R S M T D Y U I P U E R T O R I C O M N B V C X Z A L
A Q A Z E X S W E R T Y U L M N B V C X Z E B W E R T V
G R T T Y X O I U B A R B U D A M N B V C X Z E A S D A
U W I C H A I T I R E W Q C P O I U Y T R E W Q L K K D
A N P O I U Y C Y T D O M I N I C A N R E P U B L I C O
U F G H J K J H O G F D S A N T I G U A Q W E R T Y Z R
U N I T E D S T A T E S V I R G I N I S L A N D S G H E
```

Cross off the countries, departments, dependencies, and territories as you find them: Greenland, Canada, St. Pierre, Miquelon, Tobago, Mexico, Guatemala, Belize, El Salvador, Honduras, Nicaragua, Costa Rica, Panama, Bermuda, Bahamas, Cuba, Jamaica, Haiti, Puerto Rico, St. Lucia, St. Kitts, Nevis, Antigua, Barbuda, Dominica, St. Vincent, Grenadines, Barbados, Grenada, Trinidad, Dominican Republic, French Overseas Departments, British Dependencies, United States, Netherlands Dependencies, United States Virgin Islands

# Countries of North America

Use information from an atlas, encyclopedia, your geography book, or any other reference book to write two interesting facts about each North American country.

1. Antigua

   _____

   _____

2. Bahamas

   _____

   _____

3. Barbados

   _____

   _____

4. Barbuda

   _____

   _____

5. Belize

   _____

   _____

6. Bermuda

   _____

   _____

7. British Dependencies

   _____

   _____

8. Canada

   _____

   _____

9. Costa Rica

   _____

   _____

10. Cuba

    _____

    _____

11. Dominica

    _____

    _____

12. Dominican Republic

    _____

    _____

# Countries of North America *(cont.)*

13. El Salvador

_____

_____

14. French Overseas Departments

_____

_____

15. Greenland

_____

_____

16. Grenada

_____

_____

17. Grenadines

_____

_____

18. Guatemala

_____

_____

19. Haiti

_____

_____

20. Honduras

_____

_____

21. Jamaica

_____

_____

22. Mexico

_____

_____

23. Miquelon

_____

_____

24. Nevis

_____

_____

25. Netherlands Dependencies

_____

_____

# Countries of North America (cont.)

26. Nicaragua

_____

_____

27. Panama

_____

_____

28. Puerto Rico

_____

_____

29. St. Kitts

_____

_____

30. St. Lucia

_____

_____

31. St. Pierre

_____

_____

32. St. Vincent

_____

_____

33. Tobago

_____

_____

34. Trinidad

_____

_____

35. United States

_____

_____

36. United States Virgin Islands

_____

_____

Bonus Question!

Which of these countries make up the area called Central America?

_____

_____

18

# Look at the Map

Use the numbered list of North American countries on pages 16-18 to label the map below. Write the number of each country on the map and use the list for a key.

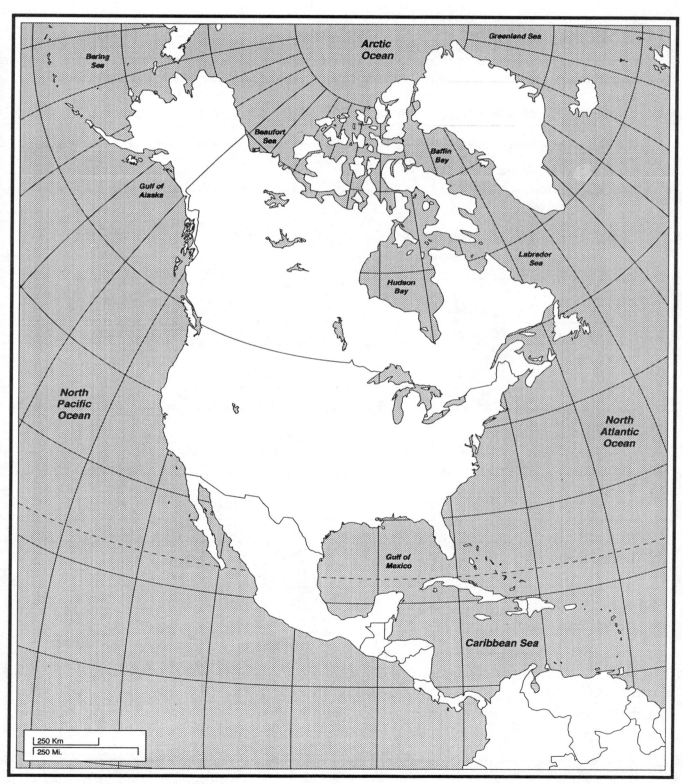

# Physical Characteristics of North America

## Major Bodies of Water

North America is surrounded by the *Atlantic Ocean* to the east, the *Pacific Ocean* to the west, the *Arctic Ocean* and the *Bering Sea* to the north, and the *Caribbean Sea* and *Gulf of Mexico* to the south.

Use reference sources to label these major bodies of water on the map of North America.

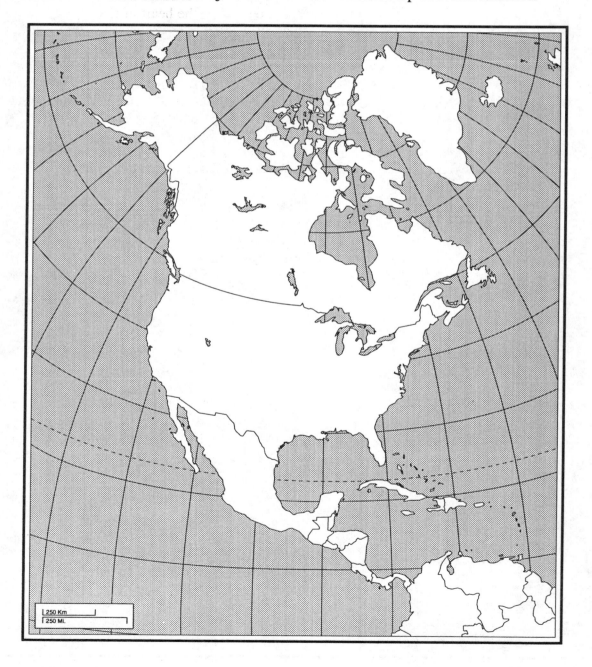

# Physical Characteristics of North America *(cont.)*

## Mountains and Plains

The three largest countries on the North American continent—the United States, Canada, and Mexico—share many physical characteristics.  The *Coast Range* runs along the Pacific coast, stretching from Northern Canada all the way through Mexico to the southern tip of Baja California.  The *Rocky Mountains* run from northern Alaska almost all the way to Mexico where another range, the *Sierra Madre Occidental*, continues until it surrounds a high plateau in the heart of that country.  The *Appalachian Mountains* start in Newfoundland and continue into the southern United States.

The *Great Basin* lies between the Coast Range and the Rocky Mountains in the United States.  The *Great Plains* are the prairie lands that lie between the Rocky Mountains and the Appalachians in the center of the continent.  The fertile *Coastal Plain* runs along the Atlantic coast and around the Gulf of Mexico.

Use reference books to label these physical characteristics on the map of North America.

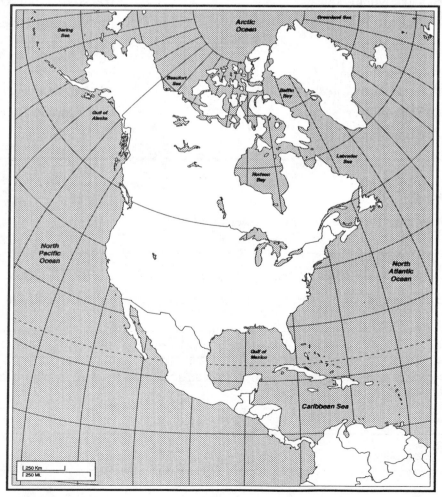

# Physical Characteristics of North America *(cont.)*

## Lakes and Rivers

Both Canada and the United States have many lakes and rivers. Four of the five *Great Lakes* form part of the border between these two countries. Only one of Mexico's major rivers is listed below. It forms part of that country's border with the United States. Also, a small stretch of the *Colorado River* flows through Mexico, dividing the Baja California peninsula from the rest of that country.

Using reference sources and the map on page 23, draw the lakes and rivers listed below. Then label those rivers and the other bodies of water with their numbers and use the list for a key.

| | |
|---|---|
| 1. Lake Superior | 12. Yukon River |
| 2. Lake Huron | 13. Mackenzie River |
| 3. Lake Erie | 14. Nelson River |
| 4. Lake Ontario | 15. St. Lawrence River |
| 5. Lake Michigan | 16. Mississippi River |
| 6. Hudson Bay | 17. Missouri River |
| 7. Lake Winnipeg | 18. Ohio River |
| 8. Great Slave Lake | 19. Tennessee River |
| 9. Great Bear Lake | 20. Arkansas River |
| 10. Snake River | 21. Colorado River |
| 11. Columbia River | 22. Rio Grande |

Bonus Questions!

Into what body of water does the Colorado River empty?

_____

_____

Which of the Great Lakes does not form part of the border between the United States and Canada?

_____

_____

The Great Lakes can be reached by ship from the Atlantic Ocean by way of which river?

_____

_____

# Physical Characteristics of North America *(cont.)*

## Lakes and Rivers

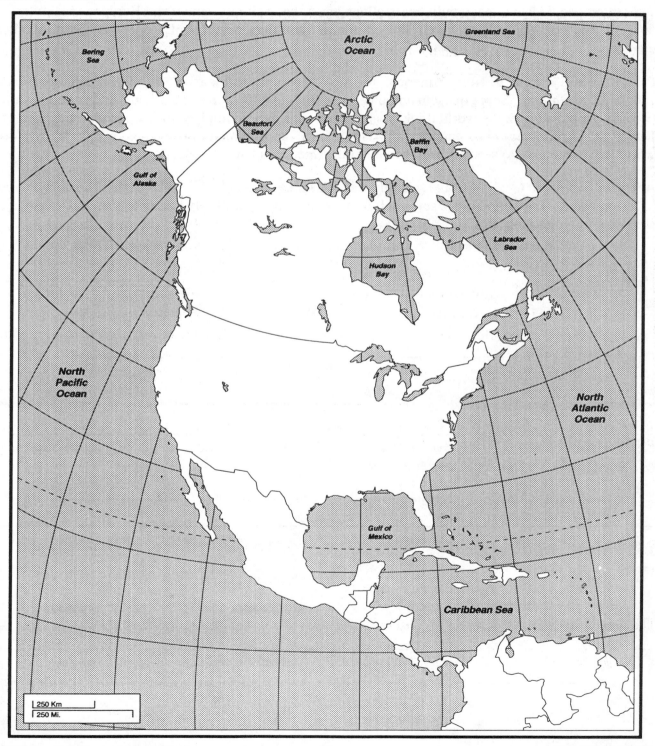

# People in North America

Everyone who lives in North America is either an immigrant or the descendant of an immigrant. Even the people who are called Native Americans are thought to have come to the Americas from Asia. Scientists think that the ocean levels were low enough during the Ice Ages to have exposed a land bridge across the Bering Strait between the areas that are now known as Russia and Alaska.

These first people had already built civilizations when the explorers came from Europe to claim the land for their countries. They were followed in turn by settlers, first from Europe and then from other continents.

People are still coming to North America. Most of them come as the result of wars, persecution, and economic hard times. Some of them come because their families are already here. Many people come because people all over the world think of North America as a good place to live. Both Canada and the United States have very high standards of living. Since the invention of television, people all over the world have been able to see how well some North Americans live.

Ask your parents to help you make a family tree. A family tree is a kind of chart that shows who your ancestors were. Try to find out where each of the people on your family tree was born and when he or she came to North America.

_____

your name

_____    _____
mother                                           father

_____  _____  _____  _____
grandmother (mother)    grandfather (mother)    grandmother (father)    grandfather (father)

_____  _____  _____  _____
great grandmother (mother)  great grandfather (mother)  great grandmother (father)  great grandfather (father)

_____  _____  _____  _____
great grandmother (mother)  great grandfather (mother)  great grandmother (father)  great grandfather (father)

# People in North America *(cont.)*

Three groups of Indians built great civilizations in the Americas before European explorers came. Two of these civilizations were located in North America. Do some research to find out something about the Aztec and the Maya civilizations.

## The Aztecs

_____

_____

_____

_____

_____

_____

_____

_____

## The Maya

_____

_____

_____

_____

_____

_____

_____

_____

# Animals in North America

Read the clues and unscramble the names of the North American animals.

1. _____ a large, horned, grazing mammal that lives in the northern part of North America (somoe)

2. _____ a small animal with mask-like markings on its face (aconor)

3. _____ a large, white, furry mammal that lives in the frozen Arctic (proal rabe)

4. _____ small rodents that dig their burrows in the grassy plains (pirerai sodg)

5. _____ a poisonous snake that warns of its approach by making a noise with its tail (altterskane)

6. _____ a reptile that has been hunted for its skin (gaillarot)

7. _____ an animal that is covered with sharp quills (ciepuporn)

8. _____ the correct name for the animal that used to roam the prairies in large herds (snoib)

9. _____ the common name for the animal that used to roam the prairies in large herds (falubof)

10. _____ a woodland animal that has antlers (rede)

11. _____ a sure-footed horned animal that romps around in the Canadian Rockies (nutonaim toga)

12. _____ a large ferocious bear that lives in the American northwest (zigryzl raeb)

13. _____ the original dam builder (raveeb)

14. _____ a small animal that hides nuts in trees and in holes in the ground (rilsquer)

15. _____ a four-footed meat eater that runs in packs (flow)

16. _____ a poisonous insect found in the deserts (pircoons)

17. _____ a poisonous lizard (gali stormen)

18. _____ a large hairy spider (alatuntar)

19. _____ a bird that is famous as the symbol of the United States (dabl glaee)

20. _____ an aquatic mammal (ase onli)

# People Depend on the Environment

Make a list of North America's natural resources.

_____

_____

_____

_____

_____

Then create a symbol to go with each natural resource and make a key.  Using your newly created symbols, show these resources on the map of North America on the next page.

## Resource Key

# People Depend on the
# Environment *(cont.)*

## Resource Map

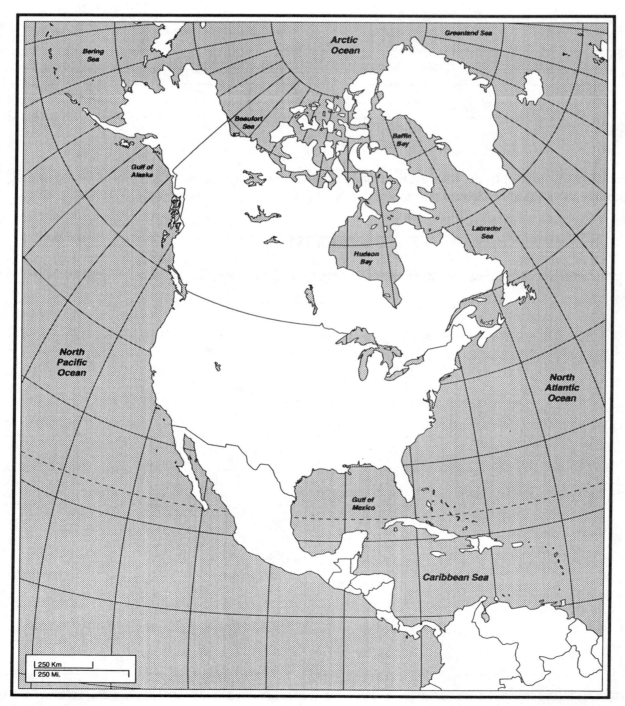

28

# People Adapt to and Change the Environment

People adapt to and change the environment in many ways. Think of some possible solutions that may solve these environmental problems:

Very dry conditions for farming:

_____

_____

_____

_____

Hills too steep for crops:

_____

_____

_____

_____

Areas that flood:

_____

_____

_____

_____

Housing in hot climates:

_____

_____

_____

_____

# People Adapt to and Change the Environment *(cont.)*

People adapt to and change the environment in many ways. Think of some possible solutions that may solve these environmental problems:

Housing in cold climates:

_____

_____

_____

_____

Clothing in hot climates:

_____

_____

_____

_____

Clothing in cold climates:

_____

_____

_____

_____

Transportation in mountainous or hilly areas:

_____

_____

_____

_____

# Technology Impacts the Environment

Resources are things valued and used by people. Natural resources are resources that occur in nature, such as minerals in the Earth, trees, water, and air.

The way people feel about and use natural resources changes as new technologies are developed.

Research the use of natural resources and how they have changed society in North America. How may natural resources change society in the future?

| Type of Resource | Past | Present | Future |
|---|---|---|---|
| **Fuel for heating** | | | |
| **Fuel for ships** | | | |
| **Fuel for trains** | | | |
| **Fuel for cars** | | | |

# Technology Impacts the Environment *(cont.)*

| Type of Resource | Past | Present | Future |
|---|---|---|---|
| **Materials for building** | | | |
| **Materials for containers** | | | |
| **Propellant for spray cans** | | | |
| **Material for paper** | | | |
| **Treatment of the air** | | | |
| **Use of water** | | | |

32

# Movement Demonstrates Interdependence

Why do human activities require movement? _____

_____

_____

Do the people in your family go places?_____Choose two people and answer the following questions:

|  | Person #1 | Person #2 |
|---|---|---|
| **Who?** |  |  |
| **When?** |  |  |
| **Where?** |  |  |
| **How far?** |  |  |
| **How often?** |  |  |
| **Why?** |  |  |
| **Mode of transportation?** |  |  |

       #693 North America

# Movement Demonstrates Interdependence *(cont.)*

Use reference sources to figure the distances between these North American cities.

**Los Angeles/New York** _____

**San Francisco/Quebec** _____

**Vancouver/Detroit** _____

**Seattle/San Diego** _____

**Edmonton/Calgary** _____

**Washington, D.C./Miami** _____

**Houston/Denver** _____

**Miami/Nassau** _____

**Dallas/Mexico City** _____

**Atlanta/Philadelphia** _____

**New York/Puerto Rico** _____

**Portland, Oregon/Portland, Maine** _____

New York 1750 km.

Denver 890 km.

Quebec 2030 km.

Mexico City 2200 km.

# Movement Involves Linkages

List several different ways people traveled in years past from place to place in North America.

_____

_____

_____

_____

_____

_____

List several different ways people travel today from place to place in North America.

_____

_____

_____

_____

_____

_____

Bonus Question!

Why do you think methods of transportation changed?

_____

_____

_____

_____

_____

# Movement Involves Linkages *(cont.)*

How will people travel around North America in the future?

_____

_____

_____

_____

Design your own future method of transportation.  Explain it and then draw a picture of it below.

_____

_____

_____

_____

This Is How My Future Transportation Will Work:

_____

_____

_____

This Is How My Future Transportation Will Look:

```
┌───────────────────────────────────────────────┐
│                                                 │
│                                                 │
│                                                 │
│                                                 │
│                                                 │
│                                                 │
│                                                 │
│                                                 │
└───────────────────────────────────────────────┘
```

# Movement Includes People, Ideas, and Products

People go places for business and for pleasure.  Going somewhere for pleasure is called touring.

Where have you gone for pleasure?

_____

_____

_____

_____

Where would you like to go?

_____

_____

_____

_____

Ideas can travel too.  List some of the different ways ideas travel from place to place.

_____

_____

_____

_____

Products also travel.  What are some of the ways products travel?

_____

_____

_____

_____

_____

# Movement Includes People, Ideas, and Products *(cont.)*

Think about one of the places you would like to spend your vacation. Design a cover for a travel brochure about that place. Sketch your design below. Write a description of the place that will make other people want to travel there too.

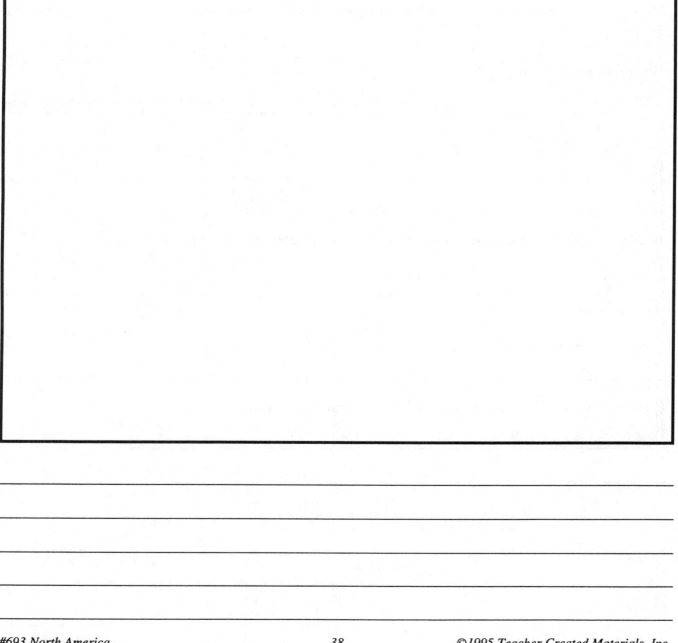

_____

_____

_____

_____

# The Far North

## Arctic Plants

A region is a portion of the Earth's surface that has characteristics unlike any other. The far north is considered its own region. You may think it is similar to Antarctica at the South Pole because of the cold, ice and snow, and the auroras, which look like dazzling light shows in the sky. However, it is quite different.

The far north is mostly ocean. This makes it less cold than the Antarctic and friendlier to animal and plant life. During the short summer of the northern region, some of the land that borders the Arctic Ocean becomes warm and thaws. This thawing allows a variety of different kinds of plants to grow; these plants include: mosses, lichen, algae, and hundreds of kinds of flowering plants. However, only the top few inches (cm) of this land thaws out, and the roots of these plants cannot penetrate below the permafrost which is the permanently frozen ground.

Several of these Arctic plants are very beautiful. Find a picture of one in a reference book and sketch it below. Be sure to write the plant's name below your sketch.

# The Far North *(cont.)*

## Animals Across the Curriculum

Many animals live in the Arctic. The *walrus*, *polar bear*, and *narwhal* are true animals of the ice floes and the icy ocean. Still more animals live on the tundra, the huge land mass that circles the North Pole, extending from the edge of the northern forests to the shores of the Arctic Ocean. The *barren-ground grizzly*, *snowy owl*, *ptarmigan*, and *lemming* share their tundra home with the *musk ox*, *caribou*, and such waterfowl as the *Canada goose*.

1. **The Walrus**

Be ready to report on the walrus. Find out what this animal eats, if it migrates, and if its territory has become smaller. Write down any other facts that you think are interesting.

_____

_____

_____

_____

_____

_____

_____

2. **The Polar Bear**

Write a poem about the polar bear. This is an animal with no natural enemies. It is hunted only by people. It may live its whole life without setting foot on land. Try to see a video tape or read an illustrated book about this bear before you write your poem.

_____

_____

_____

_____

_____

_____

# The Far North *(cont.)*

## Animals Across the Curriculum *(cont.)*

3. Put the names of the italicized animals on page 40 in ABC order and tell how many are syllables in each of the names.

_____     _____

_____     _____

_____     _____

_____     _____

_____     _____

4. **The Lemming**

   What story is told about the habits of lemmings? Do scientists still think it is true? What facts are known about lemmings?

_____

_____

_____

_____

_____

_____

_____

_____

_____

_____

# The Far North *(cont.)*

## Animals Across the Curriculum *(cont.)*

5.  **The Narwhal**
    The Narwhal is a very strange animal.  Find out about it.  What legend is associated with it?
    Write your own legend about the narwhal.  Call your legend "Why The Narwhal
    Has_____."

_____

_____

_____

_____

_____

_____

_____

_____

_____

_____

_____

_____

_____

_____

_____

_____

_____

_____

# The Far North *(cont.)*

## Animals Across the Curriculum *(cont.)*

6. **The Penguin**

    This cold-weather animal is often associated with the far north in stories. Where does it really live? Is it an Arctic animal? It is a bird, but can it fly? How does it get around? Find five more facts about the penguin.

    _____

    _____

    _____

    _____

7. A Bar Graph

    Make a bar graph comparing the features of the Arctic with the features of the Antarctic. Keep track of your facts here as you do your research.

| Features | Arctic | Antarctica |
|---|---|---|
| **High temperatures** | | |
| **Low temperatures** | | |
| **Thickness of ice** | | |
| **Varieties of plant life** | | |
| **Varieties of animal life** | | |

# Central America

Central America is the name given to the tapering isthmus that connects Mexico with South America. It is divided into seven countries. Six of them share a Spanish and Native Indian background. One of them is believed to have been founded by shipwrecked British sailors and has connections with the English-speaking island nations in the Caribbean Sea.

Find these nations in reference books and answer these questions.

1. What is the largest city in Central America?

   _____

2. In which country will you find the Maya ruin of Tikal?

   _____

3. Which country is supposed to have been founded by shipwrecked British sailors?

   _____

4. What is El Salvador's chief crop?

   _____

5. What is the poorest and least developed country in Central America?

   _____

6. What name is given to the Caribbean shore of Nicaragua?

   _____

7. Which country has the canal that links the Atlantic and Pacific Oceans?

   _____

# Central America *(cont.)*

8. Which Central American country has done away with its armed forces?

   _____

9. With which country are the Sandinista rebels associated?

   _____

10. Which Central American country has the smallest population?

    _____

11. Which country was founded because of the discovery of silver?

    _____

12. Which country has the highest literacy rate in Central America?

    _____

13. What is the capital city of each Central American Country?

    Guatemala _____

    Belize _____

    El Salvador _____

    Honduras _____

    Nicaragua _____

    Costa Rica _____

    Panama _____

# Central America *(cont.)*

Do some research on the building of the Panama Canal and write a short report about it. Find out who built it, why it was built in Panama, how long it took to build, how much it cost, and the dangers and problems that were overcome in building it.

## The Panama Canal

_____

_____

_____

_____

_____

_____

_____

_____

_____

_____

_____

_____

_____

_____

_____

_____

_____

_____

# North American Fact Game

This game can be played in different ways:

**Game 1**—You can use a *Jeopardy* format. Students love this and they can set it up all by themselves or with just a little help. Run the answer cards on one color of paper and the question cards on another color for easy sorting.

**Game 2**—You can make a card game like *rummy*. All the cards should be run on one color for this. Shuffle the cards and deal five to each player. Put the leftovers facedown or in the middle of the table. Players draw from the stack and discard in another stack. The object of the game is to lay down pairs by matching questions and answers. You can make it more complicated by allowing students to challenge one another's matched pairs if they think the matches are incorrect. Have students keep track of the rules they make and write game directions.

## Fact Game Cards

| | |
|---|---|
| It is the area where the North Pole is located. | What is the Arctic? |
| These falls are between New York, USA, and Ontario, Canada. | What is Niagara Falls? |
| The soil is permanently frozen in these Arctic plains. | What is tundra? |

## Fact Game Cards *(cont.)*

| | |
|---|---|
| These mountains extend through the western United States and Canada. | What are the Rockies? |
| These five lakes lie between the United States and Canada. | What are the Great Lakes? |
| Hawaiians wear these wreaths of flowers. | What is a lei? |
| Ottawa is the capital of this country. | What is Canada? |
| This abbreviation stands for the United States of America. | What is USA? |
| This huge canyon was formed by the Colorado River. | What is the Grand Canyon? |

# North American Fact Game (cont.)

## Fact Game Cards (cont.)

| | |
|---|---|
| This is the northernmost state in the USA. | What is Alaska? |
| This is a name commonly give to the countries that lie between Mexico and South America. | What is Central America? |
| This state belongs to the United States, but it lies in the middle of the Pacific Ocean. | What is Hawaii? |
| This is the highest point in North America. | What is Mt. McKinley? |
| This is the lowest point in North America. | What is Death Valley, California? |
| This canal connects the Atlantic and Pacific Oceans. | What is the Panama Canal? |

# North American Fact Game (cont.)

## Fact Game Cards (cont.)

| | |
|---|---|
| This North American capital city is one mile above sea level. | What is Denver, Colorado? |
| These two states in the U.S. are not connected to the other 48 states. | What are Alaska and Hawaii? |
| This North American country is the largest in land area. | What is Canada? |
| This city is the capital of the United States of America. | What is Washington, D.C.? |
| This is the capital city of Nicaragua. | What is Managua? |
| This river forms part of the border between Mexico and the U.S. | What is the Rio Grande? |

# North American Fact Game *(cont.)*

## Fact Game Cards *(cont.)*

Let your students make their own question-and-answer fact cards. Students usually like to make extra hard ones in hopes of stumping each other, so have them write the book and page number where the information can be found for each card.

| | |
|---|---|
| | Book:_____<br><br>Page: _____ |
| | Book:_____<br><br>Page: _____ |
| | Book:_____<br><br>Page: _____ |
| | Book:_____<br><br>Page: _____ |
| | Book:_____<br><br>Page: _____ |

# The Geography Center

## Putting the Center Together

You can set up your Geography Center in a corner of your classroom and make it as simple or as elaborate as you want. The center should have a map, a globe, and an atlas. (Several maps, a couple of globes, and multiple copies of the atlas would be even better.) A table and chairs will facilitate group activities and discussions. A supply of writing and drawing materials will also come in handy. A bookcase, shelf, or window sill can be utilized for storing reference books. The more reference books you can provide, the better the assigned projects will be. If you have access to a TV, VCR, and tapes, you can show movies about the places you are studying. There are many tapes of this variety available, and the visual learners in your class will really appreciate this. Cushions for sitting on the floor to read or view tapes add a cozy touch.

## Making the Center Work

You can make the Geography Center part of your instructional day by scheduling groups to do center work. Change the materials daily or weekly or provide a set of task cards at the beginning of the unit and expect each student to work through them individually or as part of a group. (See pages 53–55.)

## Use Portfolios

Have students make portfolios and store them in containers in an accessible area of your center. Try using the inexpensive but sturdy plastic crates that are available at local hardware stores. Make students responsible for their own progress by having them file their own work, both completed work and work in progress. Have students create attractive covers for their portfolios so the accumulated work can be attractively displayed at your school's open house.

## Deck the Walls

Encourage artwork, creative writing, and exploratory math to go along with your geography unit and spread it throughout the curriculum. Display these products on a bulletin board in your Geography Center. Have students mount and post their own work. They can cut out letters and create colorful captions for the board.

Have another bulletin board reserved for posting newspaper and magazine articles dealing with the continent you are studying. Encourage your students to bring in these articles, share them, and discuss their meaning and importance.

# The Geography Center (cont.)

## Task Cards

**Task Card #3**

What is the highest mountain peak on the continent?

How tall is it?

In which country is it found?

**Task Card #4**

What is the largest country on the continent?

What countries or bodies of water border it?

What is its capital city?

**Task Card #1**

What is the longest river on the continent?

How long is it?

Through which country or countries does it flow?

**Task Card #2**

What is the most important mountain range on the continent?

How long is it?

In which country or countries are these mountains found?

# The Geography Center *(cont.)*

**Task Cards** *(cont.)*

**Task Card #5**

What is the smallest country on the continent?

What countries or bodies of water border it?

What is its capital city?

**Task Card #6**

What is the largest lake on the continent?

In which country or countries is it found?

Which river is associated with it?

**Task Card #7**

What animals are associated with the continent?

In what country or countries do they live?

Are they in any danger in today's civilization?

**Task Card #8**

What variations in climate are found on the continent?

What variations in weather are found on the continent?

Can people live in all parts of the continent?

# The Geography Center *(cont.)*

## Task Card Response

Leave a stack of these task card response forms in the geography center for students to use.

Name _____ Date_____

Task Card #_____

Question #1

_____

_____

_____

_____

Question #2

_____

_____

_____

_____

Question #3

_____

_____

_____

_____

Bonus

I also learned_____

_____

_____

_____

# The Culminating Activity: Making a Book

## Method

You and your students can go about bookmaking in many different ways. Here are some suggestions:

- The book can be your students' showcase portfolios.

- Students can review and reflect upon the work they have accumulated in their portfolios, select the most representative samples or the pieces they like best, and put these things together in book form.

- The book can be a showcase portfolio based on the teacher's criteria.

- Have students select work from their portfolios, based on a list you develop.

- The book can be comprised of new material that sums up the unit.

- Have students complete various assignments meant specifically for inclusion in their books, showing their grasp of the material. (See pages 57–67.)

## Contents

In most cases you will probably want your students to include maps, facts about both physical and political geography, research about animals, people, and resources. They can review or report on any books they have read about the continent, and they can write about what they have learned and how it has affected the way they view the world.

## Cover

You can specify and provide the design for the cover so that all of the books will be uniform, or you can encourage your students to design a cover that is representative of the continent. A collage of pictures cut from magazines and travel brochures is an option that works well.

Be sure to laminate the finished covers so the books can be used as part of your classroom library or Geography Center reference shelf. Your students may also want to share their books with students in other classes.

Exciting ideas for binding and publishing follow on pages 68–70.

# The Culminating Activity: Making a Book *(cont.)*

Trace an outline map of North America. Transfer information about its physical features from all of the maps you have made. You might want to use different colors to create a key.

Name _____ Date_____

## Map of Physical Features

# The Culminating Activity:
# Making a Book *(cont.)*

Use the information you have already gathered or do some new research to complete this page.

Name _____ Date_____

## Facts About Physical Features

Area: _____

_____

Highest Point: _____

_____

Lowest Point: _____

_____

Largest Island:_____

_____

Longest River:_____

_____

Largest Lake: _____

_____

Tallest Waterfall: _____

_____

Largest Desert: _____

_____

Longest Reef: _____

_____

# The Culminating Activity: Making a Book *(cont.)*

Trace an outline map of North America. Transfer the information about its political features from all of the maps you have made. You might want to use a numbered list to create a key.

Name _____ Date_____

## Map of Political Features

# The Culminating Activity: Making a Book *(cont.)*

Use the information you have already gathered or do some new research to complete this page.

Name _____ Date_____

## Facts About Political Features

Population: _____

Largest Country (by area): _____

Largest Country (by population): _____

Smallest Country (by area): _____

Smallest Country (by population): _____

Largest Metropolitan Area (by population):_____

_____

_____

_____

_____

_____

Newest Countries:_____

_____

_____

_____

_____

_____

# The Culminating Activity: Making a Book *(cont.)*

Use the information you have already gathered or do some new research to complete this page.

Name _____ Date_____

## The People

The people of this continent belong to these ethnic groups:

_____

_____

_____

They speak these languages:

_____

_____

_____

They live in these different environments:

_____

_____

_____

_____

Their ways of life have changed or are changing:

_____

_____

_____

_____

_____

# The Culminating Activity: Making a Book *(cont.)*

Pick the city on the continent that is most interesting to you.  Use the information you have already gathered or do some new research to complete this page.

Name _____Date_____

### The city of_____.

This city is in _____

Area: _____

Population: _____

_____

Language(s): _____

_____

Ethnic Groups: _____

_____

Religious Groups: _____

_____

Famous Natural Features: _____

_____

_____

Famous Constructed Features: _____

_____

_____

_____

_____

# The Culminating Activity: Making a Book *(cont.)*

Use the information you have already gathered or do some new research to complete this page.

Name _____Date_____

## The Animals

The best known animals of this continent are _____

_____

_____

The animals of this continent are important because _____

_____

_____

The animals that still live in their natural habitats are _____

_____

_____

The animals that are on the endangered list are_____

_____

_____

_____

They are on the endangered list because _____

_____

_____

_____

_____

_____

# The Culminating Activity: Making a Book *(cont.)*

Keep track of the books you read about the continent on this log.

Name _____ Date_____

## Book Log

Title: _____    Fiction: _____

Author: _____    Nonfiction: _____

Illustrator: _____    Rating:_____

Title: _____    Fiction: _____

Author: _____    Nonfiction: _____

Illustrator: _____    Rating:_____

Title: _____    Fiction: _____

Author: _____    Nonfiction: _____

Illustrator: _____    Rating:_____

Title: _____    Fiction: _____

Author: _____    Nonfiction: _____

Illustrator: _____    Rating:_____

# The Culminating Activity: Making a Book *(cont.)*

Use copies of this form to review your favorite nonfiction books about the continent you have been studying.

Name _____ Date_____

## Book Review/Nonfiction

Title: _____

Author: _____

Illustrator: _____

Summary: _____

_____

_____

_____

_____

_____

Reasons I liked or did not like this book:_____

_____

_____

_____

_____

_____

Bonus!

If you liked this book and think other people should read it, you can do one of two things. (1) Write a paragraph or two telling how a nonfiction book can help you understand a continent or a country and post it on the bulletin board in the Geography Center. (2) Make a poster advertising the book and post it on the bulletin board in the Geography Center.

# The Culminating Activity: Making a Book *(cont.)*

Use copies of this form to review your favorite fiction books about the continent you have been studying.

Name _____ Date_____

## Book Review/Fiction

Title: _____

Author: _____

Illustrator: _____

Summary: _____

_____

_____

_____

_____

_____

Reasons I liked or did not like this book:_____

_____

_____

_____

_____

_____

Bonus!

If you liked this book and think other people should read it, you can do one of two things. (1) Write a paragraph or two telling how a fiction book can help you understand a continent or a country and post it on the bulletin board in the Geography Center. (2) Make a poster advertising the book and post it on the bulletin board in the Geography Center.

# The Culminating Activity:
# Making a Book *(cont.)*

Write a reflective essay in which you discuss the ways that studying geography has given you a better understanding of the world and the people in it.

Name _____ Date_____

**Title:**_____

_____

_____

_____

_____

_____

_____

_____

_____

_____

_____

_____

_____

_____

_____

_____

_____

_____

_____

_____

_____

_____

# The Culminating Activity: Making a Book *(cont.)*

## Book Binding Ideas

1. Stack all the pages of the book in a neat pile.

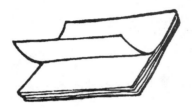

2. Place a blank sheet of paper on the top and bottom of the pages.

3. Leaving approximately 1/2" (1.25 cm) border, staple or sew all of the pages together on the left side.

4. Place two pieces of lightweight cardboard side by side. (Cereal boxes work well.) Each piece should be 1/2 to 1" (1.25 to 2.5 cm) larger than the size of the pages in the book.

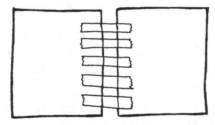

5. Leaving approximately 1" (2.5 cm) between them, tape the cardboard pieces together.

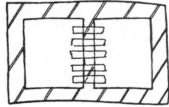

6. Put the cardboard on top of your covering material (e.g., fabric, wallpaper, contact paper, or wrapping paper). Glue the cardboard and covering material together, leaving a 1 to 1 1/2" (2.5 to 3.25 cm) material border.

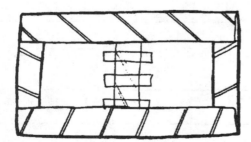

7. Fold up the edges of material over the cardboard and glue in place.

8. Glue the blank pages to the inside of the cardboard covers. Your book is ready to read and share.

68

# The Culminating Activity: Making a Book *(cont.)*

## Pop-Up Books

1. Fold a 8 1/2" x 11" (22 cm x 28 cm) piece of paper in half crosswise.

2. Measure and mark 2 3/4" (7 cm) from each side along the fold.  Cut 2 3/4" (7 cm) slits at the marks.

3. Push cut area inside-out and crease to form the pop-up section.

4. Draw, color, and cut out the object to get "popped-up."

5. Glue it onto the pop-up section.

6. Glue two pages back to back, making sure the pop-up section is free.

7. Glue additional pages together, making as many pages (including pop-up pages) as you like.  Be sure to include a free sheet on both the front and back so that those pages can be glued to a cover.

8. Glue a cover over the entire book.

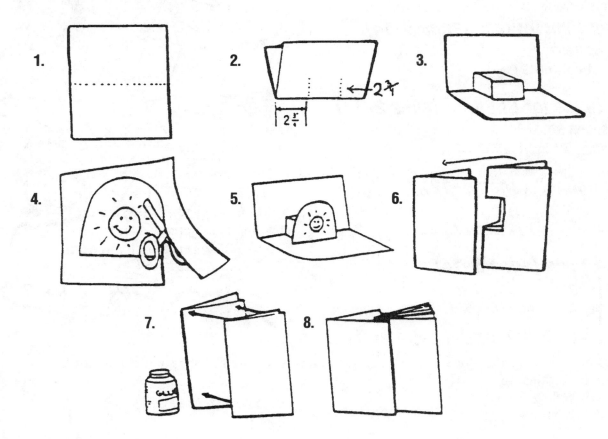

# The Culminating Activity: Making a Book *(cont.)*

## Real Markets for Student Writing

Student writing can be sent to the following addresses. Check your professional journals for more sources.

### Children's Playmate (ages 5–8)

P.O. Box 567B
Indianapolis, Indiana 46206

### Cricket (ages 6–12)

Cricket League
P.O. Box 300
Peru, Illinois 61354

### Ebony Jr! (ages 6–12)

820 S. Michigan Avenue
Chicago, Illinois 60605

### Flying Pencil Press (ages 8–14)

P.O. Box 7667
Elgin, Illinois 60121

### Highlights for Children (ages 2–11)

803 Church Street
Honesdale, Pennsylvania 18431

### Jack and Jill (ages 8–12)

P.O. Box 567B
Indianapolis, Indiana 46206

### Stone Soup (ages 5–14)

P.O. Box 83
Santa Cruz, California 95063

## National Written and Illustrated by...

(This is an awards contest for students in all grade levels. Write for rules and guidelines.)
Landmark Editions, Inc.
P.O. Box 4469
Kansas City, Missouri 64127

# Glossary

**absolute location**—See exact location.

**altiplano**—a high plateau or valley between higher mountains; particularly the high plain where the Andes divide in Peru and Bolivia

**altitude**—the height of land above the level of the sea

**Antarctic Circle**—an imaginary circle parallel to the equator and 23 degrees 30' from the South Pole.

**aquifer**—an underground reservoir of water contained within a porous rock layer

**archipelago**—a group or chain of islands

**Arctic Circle**—an imaginary circle parallel to the equator and 23 degrees 30' from the North Pole.

**atoll**—a ring of coral islands encircling a lagoon

**axis**—an imaginary line that runs through the center of the Earth from the North Pole to the South Pole

---

**basin**—an area of land that is surrounded by higher land

**bay**—a body of water having land on at least two sides

**boundary**—a line on a map that separates one country from another

---

**canal**—a waterway dug across land for ships to go through

**canyon**—a deep valley with steep sides

**cape**—a piece of land that extends into a river, lake, or ocean

**cardinal directions**—the four main points of the compass: north, south, east, and west

**cargo**—a load of products carried from one place to another

**cartographer**—a map maker

**channel**—a waterway between two land masses; also, the part of a river that is deepest and carries the most water

**climate**—the kind of weather a region has over a long period of time

**communication**—the sending out of ideas and information; the means by which people do this

**compass rose**—the drawing that shows the directions of north, south, east, and west on a map

**conservation**—preserving valuable resources

**continent**—one of the seven main land masses on the earth's surface: North America, South America, Europe, Asia, Africa, Australia, and Antarctica

**continental divide**—the geographic area that separates the direction in which water currents flow

**continental shelf**—the shallow, gently sloping sea floor that surrounds each continent

**country**—the territory of a nation, marked by a boundary that separates it from other nations

**current**—a fast-moving stream of water in the ocean

**degree**—one 360th part of the circumference of a circle; used as a unit of measurement

**delta**—an area of silt, sand, and gravel deposited at the mouth of a river

**deposit**—a large area of mineral deep in the Earth

**desert**—a very dry area of land covered with rocks and/or sand

**distance scale**—a measuring line on a map that helps to figure out the distance from one place to another

**dormant volcano**—a temporarily inactive volcano

**drought**—a long period without rain

**economic activity**—a way that people use their resources to live

**ecosystem**—a system formed by the interaction of living organisms with each other and with their environment

**environment**—the surroundings in which everything lives

**equator**—the imaginary line that circles the middle of the earth, halfway between the North Pole and the South Pole

**erosion**—the wearing away of land by the elements (ice, sun, water, and wind)

**escarpment**—a cliff separating two nearly flat land surfaces that lie at different levels

**estuary**—the widening mouth of a river where it meets the sea; tides ebb and flow within this area

**exact location**—the location of a point which can be given in latitude and longitude, also called absolute location

**extinct volcano**—a totally inactive volcano

**fertile**—good for growing plants and crops

**fjord**—a narrow, steep-sided ocean inlet that reaches far into a coastline

**forest**—a large area covered with trees and undergrowth

**frontier**—land that is mostly unsettled

**geothermal power**—energy from heat within the Earth

**geyser**—a hot spring that shoots water and steam into the air

# Glossary *(cont.)*

**glacier**—a large, thick, slow moving mass of ice

**globe**—a round model of the Earth

**gorge**—a deep, narrow passage between mountains

**grassland**—a wide area covered with grass and an occasional tree

**grid**—a series of evenly spaced lines used to locate places on a map

**grove**—a large field of trees

**growing season**—the period of time in which the weather is warm enough for crops to grow

**gulf**—an area of sea that is partly surrounded by land

---

**H**

**harbor**—a body of water sheltered by natural or artificial barriers and deep enough to moor ships

**hemisphere**—half of a sphere; on a globe, a hemisphere represents one half of the Earth

**highland**—an area of hills or mountains

**humid**—moist or damp

**hurricane**—a fierce storm of wind and rain

**hydroelectric power**—electric energy produced by water power

---

**I**

**iceberg**—a huge chunk of ice floating in the sea

**ice sheet**—a broad, thick layer of glacial ice that covers a wide area

**irrigation**—supplying water to dry land through pipes, ditches, or canals

**island**—a piece of land entirely surrounded by water

**isthmus**—a narrow strip of land that connects two larger landmasses and has water on both sides

---

**J**

**jungle**—a hot, humid area of land which is overgrown with trees and other plants

---

**K**

**key**—the section that explains the symbols used on a map

---

**L**

**lagoon**—a shallow body of water that opens on the sea but is protected by a sandbar or coral reef

**lake**—a body of water completely surrounded by land

**landform**—a shape of land, such as a mountain, valley, or plateau

# Glossary *(cont.)*

**landforms map**—a map that uses colors to show the height and shape of the land; also called a contour map

**landlocked country**—a country surrounded by land without access to the sea

**landmark**—an important thing or place that stands out from everything around it

**latitude line**—an east-west line drawn parallel to the equator on a globe

**lava**—hot, liquid rock

**location**—the position of a point on the surface of the earth; can be exact or relative

**longitude line**—a north-south line drawn from pole to pole on a globe

**lowland**—a low, flat area of land

---

**manufacturing**—making finished goods from raw materials

**map**—a drawing of all or part of the earth's surface showing where things are located

**meridian**—any of the lines of longitude running north and south on a globe or map and representing a great circle of the Earth that passes through the poles

**mesa**—a broad, flat-topped landform with steep sides found in arid or semiarid regions

**mineral**—a natural occurring substance found on the earth

**mining**—the process of taking mineral deposits from the earth

**moisture**—water or other liquids in the air or on the ground; wetness

**monsoon**—a wind that produces wet and dry seasons in southern and eastern Asia

**moor**—an open expanse of rolling land covered with grass or other low vegetation

**moraine**—an accumulation of debris carried and deposited by a glacier

**mountain**—a large mass of land that rises high above the surrounding land

**mountain range**—a group or series of mountains

**mouth**—the place where a river empties into a larger body of water

---

**natural gas**—a light mineral often used for fuel; usually found near petroleum

**natural resource**—something occurring in nature that people need or want

**North Pole**—the point located at the most northern place on a globe

---

**oasis**—a place in the desert where water from underground springs allows plants to grow

**ocean**—a large body of salt water that covers much of the earth's surface

**ore**—a mixture of rock, soil, and minerals

**outback**—the remote backcountry of Australia

---

# Glossary *(cont.)*

**parallel**—any of the imaginary lines parallel to the equator and representing degrees of latitude on the Earth's surface

**peninsula**—a body of land almost completely surrounded by water

**petroleum**—an oily liquid mineral

**place**—an area having characteristics that define them and make them different from other areas

**plain**—a low, flat land area

**plateau**—an area of flat land higher than the land around it

**pollution**—damage to air, water, or land by smoke, dust, or chemicals

**population**—all of the people who live in a particular place

**population density**—the number of people living in each square mile or kilometer of an area

**port**—a place where ships can load

**prairie**—a large area of flat land covered with tall, thick grass

**preservation**—keeping things safe from damage or destruction

**prime meridian** (Greenwich Meridian)—the special longitude line that is the starting point for measuring all the other lines of longitude

**projection**—a way of transferring the features of the Earth as represented on a globe to a flat piece of paper (map); the resulting style of map

---

**rain forest**—dense forest mostly composed of broadleaved evergreens found in wet tropical regions

**ravine**—a narrow valley with steep sides

**raw material**—a material in its natural state, used for making finished goods

**reef**—a narrow ridge of rock, sand, or coral just above or below the surface of the water

**region**—an area having distinctive characteristics that make it different from the surrounding areas

**relative location**—the location of a point on the earth's surface in relation to other points

**reservoir**—a lake or pond where water is stored for future use

**resource**—a supply of valuable or useful things such as water, coal, soil, forests, or air; see natural resource

**revolution**—the movement of the Earth in orbit around the sun; one complete revolution equals a year

**river**—a large stream of water flowing in a channel

**rotation**—the movement of the earth turning on its axis; one complete rotation equals 24 hours

**rural**—away from cities and close to farms

# Glossary (cont.)

**savanna**—a tropical grassland with scattered trees

**scale**—the ratio of map distance to actual distance on the Earth's surface

**sea**—a large body of salt water

**sound**—a long, broad ocean inlet usually parallel to the coast, or a long stretch of water separating an island from the mainland

**South Pole**—the point located at the most southern place on a globe

**state**—the strongest governing body, subordinate to a national government (Not to be confused with the nation-state.)

**steppe**—a grassland in the temperate zone where limited rainfall prevents tree growth

**strait**—a narrow waterway that connects two seas

**swamp**—a lowland area covered with shallow water and dense vegetation

**symbol**—something that stands for a real thing

**temperature**—the measure of how hot or cold a place is

**territory**—a region that is owned or controlled by another country or political unit

**time zone**—one of 24 areas or zones of the Earth in which the time is one hour earlier than in the zone to its east

**tributary**—a river or stream that flows into a larger body of water

**transportation**—the way in which people or goods travel or are moved from one place to another

**Tropic of Cancer**—the parallel of latitude that lies 23 degrees 27' north of the equator

**Tropic of Capricorn**—the parallel of latitude that lies 23 degrees 27' south of the equator

**tundra**—a wide, treeless arctic plain where few plants or animals live because of frozen subsoil called permafrost

**urban sea**—the city and its surrounding built-up area

**valley**—a long, low area between hills or mountains

**volcano**—an opening in the earth's surface through which hot liquid rock (magma) and other materials are forced out

**weather**—the condition of the air at a certain time or place

# Software Review

**Software:** *The Oregon Trail* (MECC)

**Hardware:** CD-ROM player, Macintosh or IBM/Windows compatible computer (4MB)

**Grade Level:** Intermediate

**Summary:** *The Oregon Trail* is a program that simulates one of America's early pioneer movements. Your students will become the pioneers who crossed the American West by wagon train along the Oregon Trail. The Oregon Trail stretched 2,000 miles (3,200 km), starting in Independence, Missouri and ending in the Willamette Valley of the Oregon Region. Some obstacles of the trip will be to cross wild rivers, trek dangerous mountain passes, experience disease and possible starvation, cope with inclement weather, among a number of other things that can go wrong. Just like the pioneers did, your students will have to prepare for their trip, making sure they have enough food, ammunition, clothes, spare wagon parts, etc. This simulation challenges students to make difficult decisions in difficult places. Should you trade food for fresh drinking water? What kind of trade can be made for a spare wagon wheel? Should you wait for the river to subside or cross it to save time? This is a simulation of trial and error and each time your students go through it they will become better pioneers.

# Bibliography

Aylesworth, Thomas G. and Virginia L. Aylesworth. *Eastern Great Lakes: Indiana, Michigan, Ohio.* Chelsea, 1991.

Aylesworth, Thomas G. and Virginia L. Aylesworth. *Territories and Possessions: Guam, Puerto Rico, U.S. Virgin Islands, American Samoa, North Marina Islands*. Chelsea, 1992.

Berger, Gilda. *The Southeast States.* Watts, 1984.

Brickenden, Jack. *Canada.* Watts, 1989.

Bulmer, Thomas. *Journey Through Mexico.* Troll, 1990.

*Canada in Pictures*. Lerner, 1989.

Carpenter, Allan. *Far Flung America.* Childrens, 1979.

Crossland, Bert. *Where On Earth Are We?* Book Links, 1994.

Department of Geography, Lerner Publications Company Staff. *Mexico in Pictures.* Lerner, 1988.

Dickinson, Mary B. (Ed.). *National Geographic Picture Atlas of Our World.* National Geographic Society, 1993.

*Geographic Education National Implementation Project.* Guidelines, 1987.

Gilfond, Henry. *The Northeast States.* Watts, 1984.

Harrison, Ted. *O Canada.* Tickner, 1993.

Herda, D.J. *Ethnic America: The North Central States.* Millbrook, 1991.

Hicks, Peter. *The Aztecs.* Thomson, 1993.

Jacobson, Daniel. *The North Central States.* Watts, 1984.

Lawson, Don. *The Pacific States.* Watts, 1984.

LeVert, Suzanne. *Canada: Facts and Figures*. Chelsea, 1992.

LeVert, Suzanne. *Dominion of Canada.* Chelsea, 1992.

LeVert, Suzanne. *Ontario*. Chelsea, 1990.

Lourie, Peter. *Yukon River: An Adventure to the Gold Fields of the Klondike.* Boyds Mills, 1992.

McCarry, Charles. *The Great Southwest.* National Geographic, 1980.

Moran, Tom. *A Family in Mexico.* Lerner, 1987.

# Bibliography (cont.)

Meyerricks, William and Frank Ronan. *All About Our 50 States.* Random, 1978.

Reilly, Mary J. *Mexico.* Marshall Cavendish, 1991.

Smith, Eileen Latell. *Mexico: Giant of the South.* Dillon, 1983.

Stein, R. Conrad. *Mexico.* Childrens, 1984.

St. George, Judith. *The Mount Rushmore Story.* Putnam, 1985.

*The Story of America: A National Geographic Picture Atlas.* National Geographic, 1984.

## Technology

Broderbund. *MacGlobe & PC Globe and MacUSA & PC USA.* Available from Learning Services, (800) 877-9378. disk

Broderbund. *Where in the USA Is Carmen Sandiego? and Where in America's Past is Carmen Sandiego?* Available from Troll (800)526-5289. CD-ROM and disk

DeLorme Publishing. *Global Explorer.* Available from DeLorme Publishing, 1995. CD-ROM

Didatech. *Crosscountry USA.* Available from Learning Services, (800)877-9378. disk

Discis. *Great Cities of the World, Volumes 1 & 2.* Available from Learning Services, (800)877-9378. CD-ROM

Macmillan/McGraw-Hill. *U.S. Atlas Action and World Atlas Action.* Available from Learning Services, (800)877-9378. disk

MECC. *Canada Geograph II, The Oregon Trail, The Yukon Trail, and USA Geograph II.* Available from MECC, (800)685-MECC; in Canada call (800)663-7731. CD-ROM and disk

National Geographic. *Rain Forest.* Available from Educational Resources, (800)624-2936. laserdisc

Orange Cherry. *Talking U.S.A. Map.* Available from Learning Services, (800)877-9378. disk

Orange Cherry. *Time Traveler.* Available from Educational Resources, (800)624-2936. CD-ROM

Software Toolworks. *U.S. Atlas and World Atlas.* Available from Learning Services, (800)877-9378. CD-ROM and disk

SVE. *Geography on Laserdisc.* Available from Learning Services, (800)877-9378. laserdisc

Troll. *All About America, America Coast to Coast, Crosscountry Canada, Game of the States, The States Game, Time Tunnel: Early America, and U.S. Map.* Available from Troll, (800)526-5289. disk

# Answer Key

## Page 15

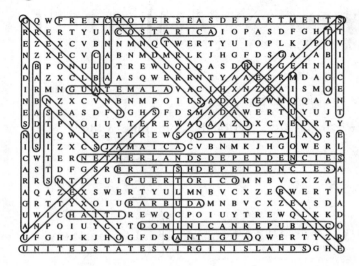

## Page 26

1. moose
2. racoon
3. polar bear
4. prairie dogs
5. rattlesnake
6. alligator
7. porcupine
8. bison
9. buffalo
10. deer
11. mountain goat
12. grizzly bear
13. beaver
14. squirrel
15. wolf
16. scorpion
17. gila monster
18. tarantula
19. bald eagle
20. sea lion

## Pages 44–45

1. Guatemala City
2. Guatemala
3. Belize
4. coffee
5. Honduras
6. The Mosquito Coast
7. Panama
8. Costa Rica
9. Nicaragua
10. Belize
11. Honduras
12. Costa Rica
13. Guatemala City

Belmopan

San Salvador

Tegucigalpa

Managua

San Jose

Panama City